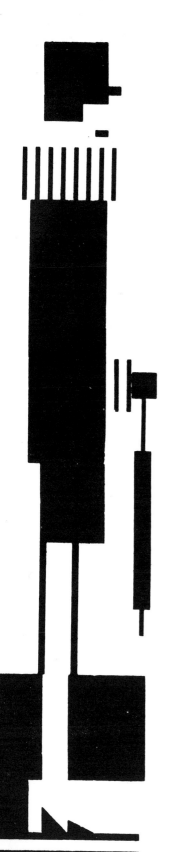

Nederland
Trademarks
1900-1950

Fifty Years of Classic Design

John Mendenhall

Art Direction Book Company
New York

Nederland Trademarks 1900-1950
Fifty Years of Classic Design
©1995 by John Mendenhall

Printed in the United States of America

Published by
Art Direction Book Company
10 East 39th Street
New York, NY 10016

ISBN 0-88108-150-7
LCC 94-079354

Other books by John Mendenhall:

American Trademarks 1930-1950, Volumes 1-3
High Tech Trademarks, Volumes 1 & 2
British Trademarks of the 1920s & 1930s
Character Trademarks
French Trademarks: The Art Deco Era
Scan This Book

Dedicated to Dan and Susan Piel,
in celebration of 15 years of friendship.

Special thanks goes to Willi Bruyns-Miller for
her invaluable assistance in translating
Dutch to English. Gratitude also to the staff
at the Netherlands Trademark Office and the
European Patent Office for their support
in the research of this book.

An early trademark for a cigar
producer featured the familiar
canalscape of Amsterdam.

Gebon, a button manufacturer,
utilized an anthropomorphic
man as its whimsical identity.

A dragon holding a flower in
this 1928 logo was a symbolic
form combining power and a
touch of humanity for
a large chemical industry.

Typography formed into people
was commonly employed in
trademarks, as in the 1927
mascot for the School voor de
Grafische Vakken te Utrecht,
a printing and design school.

For centuries **the Netherlands** has been a significant center of **trade** and **commerce** in Europe. This role took on a greater importance at the **turn of the century**, as trade with Africa and the colonies of Indonesia expanded. Trading companies imported all manner of products, but most especially coffee, tea, cocoa, and tobacco. The treidmerk (trademark) was an important image-builder for companies doing business overseas. In most instances it guaranteed uniqueness, although it was common for one company to copy the symbol of their competitor. Early trademarks were engraved illustrations which were printed with great prominence on company letterheads. Often the mark was reproduced on packaging, such as tea containers or tobacco wrappings, as a method of rapid identification for the consumer.

Many businesses other than trading companies used trademarks as identifying images for their products. The Dutch are renowned for their dairy and farm production, so a vast number of symbols at the beginning of the 1900s relate to these enterprises. Milk, cheese, vegetables, grains, and baked goods were the predominant staples indigenous to the region. As the machine age evolved, industrialization within the urban areas such as Den Haag and Rotterdam led to the start-up of many small and medium-sized factories. All types of products were manufactured after World War I, from heavy industrial equipment to consumer necessities.

Intellectually inclined, the Dutch are masters at engineering and mass-production. The Philips' Gloeilampenfabriken manufactured all types of electrical equipment for the domestic and foreign markets. After 1925, their lightbulb trademark became a ubiquitous symbol on signs, in advertising, and on packaging throughout Europe. Similarly, the Droste Company was synonymous with chocolate around the world. Their cartoon-like symbol of a little chocolate drop man is a classic. As with many trademarks, over the years it has evolved to a more abstract form.

The Dutch are also considered great shoppers, so it is not surprising to see a wide spectrum of merchants distinguish their stores with marks of variety and ingenuity. From food shops to taverns, many of the most inventive symbols were created for small businesses. A great many of these images would have passed into obscurity, had it not been for proud owners who dutifully registered their logos with the trademark office.

Prior to World War I, most trademarks from the Netherlands utilized Victorian-style illustrations. The exception were the Art Nouveau designs, which had widespread albeit short-lived popularity throughout Holland. Termed Nieuwe Kunst, this ornamental style featured curvilinear lines inspired by flower stems and vines. A common theme of trademarks in this style was the image of a young woman with long, flowing hair accompanied by equally curvaceous typography. Nieuwe Kunst borrowed from the French, German and Austrians; a few exceptional logo designs utilized a more geometric approach as developed in Vienna by the Weiner Werkstat.

Because Holland was neutral during World War I, the graphic arts industry flourished due to reduced competition. Most trademark designers worked for printers, since the graphic design profession as a separate entity did not exist in the Netherlands until the mid 1930s. Technical institutes such as Der School voor

The trademark for a bitters and elixers producer utilized a Victorian-style engraved design common in the Netherlands and Europe around the turn of the century.

After 1905 the sinuous lines of Art Nouveau began appearing in logos such as this one for a cigar manufacturer in Eindhoven.

Art Deco replaced Art Nouveau after 1925. The Philips' Gloeilampenfabrieken identity had the simplicity and geometric forms associated with this popular style.

de Grafische Vakken te Utrecht trained students in the typographic and printing arts, while offering adjunct courses in drawing, printmaking and illustration. This school in particular was responsible for promoting design; its annual yearbook fea- excellence in publicity and featured reproductions of student graphic design as well as articles on the latest trends in typesetting and print technology.

In the 1920s a revolt occurred against the excess of decoration as epito- mized by Art Nouveau. The theories of such design pioneers as J.J.P.Oud and Theo van Doesburg had a profound impact on the look of Dutch graphic design. Stripping-away of ornament reduced forms to a simpler, more direct communica- tion. The De Stijl group promoted the ideals of the so-called New Typography, based on Constructivist principles, whose influence can be seen after 1927. One of its distinguishing characteristics was the exclusive use of sans serif type, often constructed from the blocks found in a typesetter's cabinet. Other features of the New Typography were the use of hairlines and rules as integral aspects of a typo- graphic composition, the preference for asymmetrical arrangements of printed pages, and use of photomontage. The designers Piet Zwart and Paul Schuitema were the greatest exponents of this movement.

It did have its detractors. Printers who had been trained in the "Old School" of typography were put-off by the new movement's disregard for legibili- ty. The following story, entitled *A Protest Meeting*, appeared in the 1927 yearbook of Der School voor de Grafische Vakken. It gives a humorous account of an imagi- nary meeting of letterforms in Utrecht, and the discord which occurs when they discuss the advent of Constructivism in typography.

Coming from all directions, the trains rushed into the Utrecht station. Peculiar beings descended, stared at and after, with surprise or mock, by the travel crowd of the day. Long, little, thick and completely crooked figures, dressed to the nines and very simple, extremely old and very young appearing types, who had never seen each other before, but still recognized each other, and who had traveled to Utrecht for the same purpose.

DE OUD-HOLLANDSCH

A famous Utrecht professor shook his head in thought and murmured: "I've seen them sometime, but I can't remember where." To which one of the types that had just passed him nudged his companion and said: "That's Goetenbergian. Amazing, I do know him. Forty years ago his dissertation was set out of me." The twosome left through the exit and the oldest discovered immediately the flower shop of Eggink, entered and returned with a beautiful rose, which he offered gallantly to his younger travel partner with the words: "This belongs with you. I have been taken over by you, am indeed old-fashioned, but my life is not to be extinguished." They almost collided with someone who stood there with open mouth and obvious curiosity staring at the strangers.

"Say friend, would you show us the way to the Conference Center?" As if speaking to himself, the gentleman said: "The old medieval and the Dutch medieval..." "Hey, here's someone with more knowledge of letters than the professor of Dutch literature of a moment ago. Say, are you a typographer?" "Yes, but out of work," he replied. "That's fine, then you'll be our guide and guest today. Let's go to the meeting!"

Not ever before had the famous dining room in the Jaarbeurs housed such a company. Such a strange mix was not seen even at masked balls. A few hundred together and not one was the same as the other. The waiters were wondering anxiously what kind of tip they could expect from this crowd. They must have worried, as they certainly didn't hurry to take orders.

DE CURSIEF

The "old medieval" presided and opened the meeting: "Gentlemen, welcome to this beautiful city, where our services were used for the first time as early as 1473. Those were the printers Nicolaas Ketelaar and Gerard de Leempt, who published the Historia Ecleciastica by Eusebius. In 1479 the local printer was the famous Johann Veldener, known as an experienced printer in all arts of typography and related professions. We need to remember such men. I suggest we raise our glass to these three pioneers." "That's not possible, mister president, we haven't got anything yet," sounded some voices. "The service is not very fast."

"Oh, that'll happen," continued the speaker, "If the waiters see money. Let's postpone our toast until later when we'll sit down for dinner. Afterwards, we will visit the streets which carry names of our first three Utrecht printers, under guidance of our guide here, whom I'll introduce to you now as being a temporarily out of work Utrechtian typographer...What do you say, there are no such streets? How about a monument, that'll have to be somewhere...What, neither that? Well then, gentlemen, I suggest that the Council of Utrecht has made a serious omission, unless it is not a habit in this city to honor famous citizens."

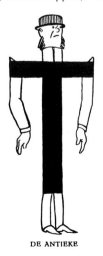

DE ANTIEKE

"Next, let us get to the purpose of our meeting. One of our colleagues, the Antique, has filed a complaint that he had been abused most awfully here in the Netherlands. Yes gentlemen, I tell you abused, and that in connection with the names he is called and how he is rendered. What is happening here in the Netherlands is a disgrace."

The speaker sheds a tear, and many regret that they did not bring a clean handkerchief. "Who wants to speak?" The Italic rises and asks why the Antique is upset. "Because one letter type feels dishonored, doesn't mean that all others need to to be involved." Loud protests are heard. "It is the treacherous Italian blood that speaks," yells a Bold. A Thin asks to speak and says that the observation of the Bold is uncalled for, that treason can come from anywhere, and that he always respected the great Italian book printer Aldus Mantius in Venice, who in the beginning of the 16th Century let Frans van Bologna cut the Italic in order to make a publication of the Virigilius appear like handwriting." Others demand to speak, but the president hammers and wishes to hear the Antique, the one with the complaint, first. He asks the Antique to climb up to the speaker's chair and present solid proof of his complaint. Under deadly silence the Antique approaches.

"Gentlemen, I am called antique, I am antique. Long before the invention of book printing, yes, even centuries before that I was found chiseled in monuments. But what have I found? My name was misused repeatedly. By different letter makers I was given another name each time. Even here in this country they use the name antique, stone letter, grotesque. I was even called butter letter by some typographers. Do I deserve that? Haven't I made myself useful through my simplicity? Which letter is to read and drawn the easiest? I pride myself of these accomplishments, although I do want to recognize other colleagues who also have good characteristics. I have suffered the sorrow of my continually changing name, but what happens currently is barbaric. I have been imitated in a most humiliating manner. I have been made up from all sorts of lines, and the results I will show you."

Some creatures, who were clad in a long coat until now, come forward and show themselves in their misshaped nudity, the letters A, B, C, M, U, X, K, N, R, S, W, and Z.

Words like "monstrous" and "revolting" are heard throughout the room, while even the Italic murmurs: "I didn't realize it was this bad." Stealthy glances are directed at the typesetter, who, although he assumes no guilt, feels uncomfortable by the hostile attitude. "And you have brought us one of the guilty ones, mister president!" cries the Egyptian all of a sudden.

The setter shudders with fear and wants to leave. "Stop!" a few letters call out, repeating the word that they have heard a printer use so often when white space got out of hand. "Stay here and face your responsibility." "You've got the word," the president tells his victim icily.

The setter gets an idea to save him from this prickly situation. He returns, and takes his place next to the president: "Gentlemen, I am very pleased that this company considers me guilty. I am out of work, and cannot find any employment anymore. How do you imagine that I could put such shoddy work together. But let me tell you, this disgraceful typesetting is done by job printers, ordered by and created by so-called artists who are possessed by Constructivism. Only a job printer who'd like to be artistic would construct such letters. I can assure you that this happens almost never. I, in my capacity as a typesetter, have never attempted this."

This report would be too long if the lengthy discussion was published here, so we'll just record the motion which was finally accepted unanimously, after having been changed many times. "The letter types, here united, voice their utmost indignation about the mockery done to one of their colleagues. They spell a curse on all who initiated the construction of letters from lines, and call the typo devil for help by deforming the setting into hopeless nonsense, and by giving the guilty type-setter such a cramp that he'll be incapable of work. Also, he who lowers himself by setting words through stacking letters on top of each other will be infected by the Chinese fever so that his eyes will change into slits and his skin will yellow like saffron, after which he will be avoided like the plague. We commit ourselves through all available means to carry out these punishments."

The president closed the meeting, after which all remained peacefully together so that our drawing teacher, Mr. Kraan, could sketch some of these letter types for this lustrum book.

With typical Dutch wit, this short story summarizes the battle between the design traditionalists and the forces of change which swept through the Netherlands during the 1930s. Typography moved from merely communicating information to being an expressive medium. Likewise in trademark design, illustrations shifted from the mere rendering of objects to expressive statements alluding to the strength and vitality of the underlying companies.

Using metaphor in graphic design is what ultimately distinguishes the profession from its origins in the purely technical trades of typesetting and printing. Dutch trademark designers made the transition from reality to illusion with enthusiasm. Images became dramatic as the Art Deco aesthetic swept through the Netherlands. Themes such as factories, gears, angular

human figures, and modes of transportation were commonly employed in trademark designs. While Holland suffered with the rest of the world through the Depression of the 1930s, these marks served as reminders of the inherent strength and determination of the Dutch spirit. The work of French designers such as Léon Dupin, A.M.Cassandre, and Jean Carlu had a profound influence on trademark designers to the north. Cubist imagery accompanied by blocky, sans serif typography became an appropriate alternative to the flowery Art Nouveau designs of the previous decades. To a lesser extent, the impact of German designers such as Karl Schulpig can be seen in some of the more geometric, impersonal forms of the mid-1930s.

While it had been traditional for printers to collaborate with artists in book design from as early as the 1880s, few Dutch companies engaged artists directly in the production of advertising or publicity design until the 1920s. Typically, a printer would be hired by a company to produce their stationery or packaging. It was generally the printer who would commission a freelance artist to draw up a logo design, which was then sold to the client.

This approach changed as awareness of design accelerated. Three companies in particular, Calvé-Delft, Van Nelle, and Bruynzeel, were at the forefront of directly commissioning artists and the new graphic design professionals. The founder of Bruynzeel, a carpentry factory, was a childhood friend with Piet Zwart and particularly enjoyed the work of the DeStijl group. Thus evolved a working relationship that lasted over thirty years and which included logo, advertising, packaging, and even yacht design.

Between the wars, the *Industries Fair* served to promote Dutch product and graphic design. Centered in Utrecht, this annual exhibition of the best in domestic and foreign work was instrumental in fueling a collaboration between art and industry. Businesses were made aware of the importance of quality design in the improvement of sales both at home and abroad. The *VANK* (Netherlands Association for Crafts and Industrial Art) and *BKI* (Dutch Association for Art and Industry) were also instrumental in encouraging beauty, as well as functionality, in design.

In 1948 another group, the *VRI* (Advertising Designers' and Illustrators' Society) was formed as a professional organization of artists and designers who were available to do creative work after the war. Membership in the VRI was obtained only after strict inquiry into the professional skill of the candidate, thus guaranteeing the work of its group to potential clients. The <u>VRI BOOK</u> was produced to showcase members' skills. Machiel Wilmink, President of the organization, stated in the book's Preface: "The growing industry and export of Dutch industrial products call for presentation and publicity on an international level. In our own country modern efficiency, production methods and salesmanship require equally modern ways of presentation, technically and artistically, suiting and appealing to the public of our day."

This attitude among Dutch graphic designers can clearly be seen in the logo designs of the first half of this century. They have energy and expressiveness, and often reflect the Dutch sense of humor in their whimsical appeal. Rarely austere, corporate identities were conceived using images of people, animals, landscapes, and letters or inanimate objects made into anthropomorphic form. They are friendly designs which lack pretension.

Viewed as cultural signposts, trademarks can give us insights into a national mood. These icons not only reflect the business climate of the Netherlands, but also suggest the fashions, interests, trends, and aspirations of the Dutch people during a vital period of their history. This collection is a tribute to the talent of the artists and designers, most working anonymously, who created so many marks of distinction.

Donszelmann & Company
Oatmeal • 1900

ELECTRISCHE KOFFIEBRANDERY

FAST COLORS

MANUFACTURED IN HOLLAND

B.P. Frankfort
Coffee roasting • 1900

Nico ter Kuile & Zonen
Cotton • 1901

DAT SMAAKT.

HAVANASIGAREN
PUIKE MARYLAND'S 2a
PER PAKJE ƒ0,40
RAPPÉ Pᴿ 500 ƒ 18
Pᴿ 1000 ƒ 35
KOFFY THEE

**Tabak, Snuif, Sigaren,
te ALMELO bij**

DE MOOR.

**G. ten Bruggencate.
Almelo.**

GEDEPONEERD

A. ter Braake
Snuff & cigars • 1901

A.M. van den Biggelaar
Tobacco & cigars • 1905

Twentsche Tabakshandel
Tobacco • 1908

16

Egeter & Company
Tobacco products • 1901

A. Hillen
Cigars & cigarettes • 1902

Rademaker's Koninklijke Chocoladefabrieken
Chocolates • 1902

Hollandsche Thee Import
Tea • 1900

A. van Beek
Cigars • 1904

C.J. Boele & Zoon
Tobacco products • 1902

P.M.F. Smolders
Cigars • 1904

Eugéne Goulmy & Baar
Cigars & cigarettes • 1906

W. van der Voet
Cigars • 1900

Gebrs. Sanders
Tobacco products • 1905

J.M. de Lange
Margarine • 1900

Albers Creameries
Margarine • 1905

L. Teurlinckx & Zoon
Cigars • 1914

J.P. Hoppenbrouwers
Cigars & cigarettes • 1909

G.W. van der Boor
Cigars • 1904

J.J. Vles & Zoon
Linoleum wax • 1904

D.G. Ruarus
Bicycles • 1908

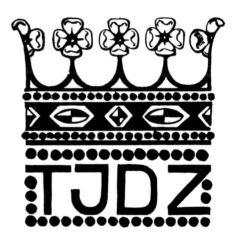

F.A. van der Aa
Bicycles • 1906

P. Cremer
Bicycles • 1909

J. Zijtstra
Coffee • 1912

Th. A. Dobbe
Writing papers • 1908

Jos. Vas Dias & Company
Lithography • 1905

Stein & Takken
Cement • 1904

J.F. Hendriks
Mattresses • 1904

Eerste Haarlemsche Gas Industrie
Gas apparatus • 1906

MORITZ·GLANS·VENUS·BRONS.

A. P. Moritz
Haircoloring • 1902

Eugéne Goulmy & Baar
Cigars • 1905

M.I. Roeg
Toiletries • 1900

L. de Gruyter
Coffee • 1902

Naaimachinenhandel
Sewing machines • 1905

Karl Stocky
Shoe polish • 1905

M.C. Verloop
Spring water • 1904

H. de Jong
Cocoa & chocolate • 1902

J.J. Onnes
Tea • 1907

Utrechtsche Cooperative
Broodbakkeri
Margarine & butter • 1907

Droste's Cocoa en Chocolade -fabrieken
Cocoa & chocolate • 1909, 1926, 1931

Le Meilleur
Tea • 1904

Stoom-Meelfabriek
Grain production • 1920

Alexander Bouwens
Cigars & cigarettes • 1900

de Vetten's Boterbiesjes
Pastries • 1914

Faddegon & Company
Printing • 1908

Gran Fabrica de Tabacos Puros
Tobacco products • 1904

A. Scholten
Cigars • 1906

E.G. Volkersz
Writing paper • 1904

Gedeponeerd

Carl Schroder
Cotton • 1912

H.B. de Beer
Wine • 1904

Nederlands Distilleries
Distilled spirits • 1910

H. de Raat Jr.
Shoe cream • 1913

D. Vaarties
Egg producer • 1917

Konin Stearnine Kaarsenfabriek
Candles • 1914

Kattenburg & Company
Clothing store • 1920

Hest & Company
Children's school • 1919

Bedum Melkfabriek
Milk • 1923

Eugéne Goulmy & Baar
Cigar packaging • 1907

Aug. Spoerl
Shoe polish label • 1912

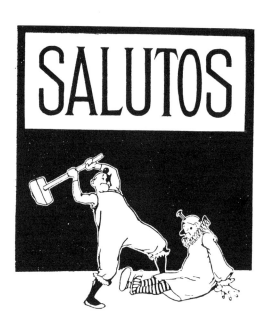

Eugéne Goulmy & Baar
Cigars • 1907

J. Baars & Zoon
Tobacco products • 1907

S. Middlekamp
Tobacco products • 1908

E.A. Muller
Tobacco products • 1908

J.H. van Hulst & Company
Tobacco products • 1910

Taconis & Wijnveldt
Cigars • 1911

R. & J.W. Hulscher
Tobacco products • 1911

H. van Toor Jzn.
Lemonade • 1911

J.L.L. Taminiau & Company
Jams • 1911

Keijzer's Theeën bestaan uit een mengsel van de beste China-Java-Ceylon-en Assam Theesoorten, die met veel zorg en vakkennis zijn gekozen, en daardoor een drank opleveren, geurig, krachtig, zeer waterhoudend, en ongeëvenaard lekker. Keijzer's Theehandel is gevestigd: Prinsengracht 180, o. d. Westermarkt AMSTERDAM.

WETTIG GEDEPONEERD

H.P. Gelderman & Zonen
Cotton • 1910

Koffie en Theehandelsvereeniging
Coffee & tea • 1920

Jurgens' Margarinefabrieken
Margarine • 1912

H. Keijzer
Tea • 1910

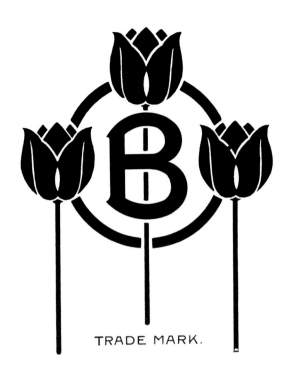

TRADE MARK.

Firma van den Berg & Zoon
Tulip bulbs • 1916

H. Burgers
Motor vehicles • 1911

Excelsior
Fabriek van Melkproducten
Milk • 1914

Sebastian Dudok van Heel
Milk • 1914

Johan Volker
Milk • 1914

Hollandsche Melkproducten
Milk • 1914

Wynand Fockink
Liqueurs • 1917

C.F. Korpershoek
Tobacco products • 1915

Eduard Huf
Cigarettes • 1913

J.H. Sommer
Shoe polish • 1910

John Paramentier
Cigarettes • 1918

A. Weurman
Cigarettes • 1911

Spaan & Bertram
Cigarettes • 1917

Gebbling & Peters
Bread & biscuits • 1913

A.J. Polak
Pudding powder • 1919

Firma Buéno & Company
Writing paper • 1918

Distilleerderij "De Tijd"
Alcoholic beverages • 1919

H.W. Massink
Alcoholic beverages • 1920

D. Meerstadt & Company
Tobacco products • 1920

Amsterdam Cooperative Sigarenwinkeliers
Tobacco products • 1923

B.M. Lieshout & Zonen
Cigars • 1923

Anton Adrianus Herfst Jr.
Cigars • 1923

D. Blazer & Hetz
Pencils • 1921

"Proco"
Consumer products • 1920

Firma Klisser & Citroen
Mechanical equipment • 1919

Hollandsche Ingenieurs
Machinery • 1919

Chemische Fabriek Solar
Paints • 1920

J.H. Sommer
Shoe preserver • 1910

L.I. Akker
Haircutters • 1918

Carbona Maatschappij
Industrial products • 1918

Erven Casper Flick
Cocoa • 1919

Henri Vlek's Wijnhandel
Barrister • 1921

D' Hollantse Damper
Tobacco products • 1923

Dassen & v.d. Meeren
Cigars • 1926

"De Waag"
Tobacco products • 1922

Frederik Herman de Groot
Tobacco products • 1924

Cohen en van der Laan
Margarine • 1923

Benschop & Company
Alcoholic beverages • 1920

Reesink & Company
Industrial products • 1922

Wolf & Hertzdahl
Clothing • 1921

Gardinge's Sigarenfabrieken
Cigars & cigarettes • 1922

Jacque Fortuin Jr.
Tobacco products • 1921

M.E. Donker
Hats • 1923

Chemische Fabriek "Yankee"
Shoe polish • 1924

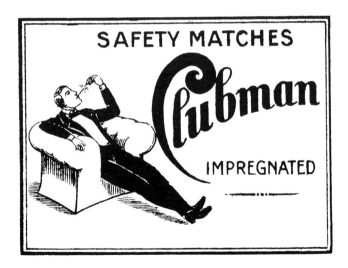

L.I. Akker
Food products • 1919

Lupowa Maatschappij
Matches • 1922

Haighton & Company
Obligatories • 1923

Herms. Oldenkott
Tobacco products • 1923

Gerson Levie
Brandzalf • 1923

Van der Werff & Company
Beds • 1925

Cohen en van der Laan
Margarine • 1923

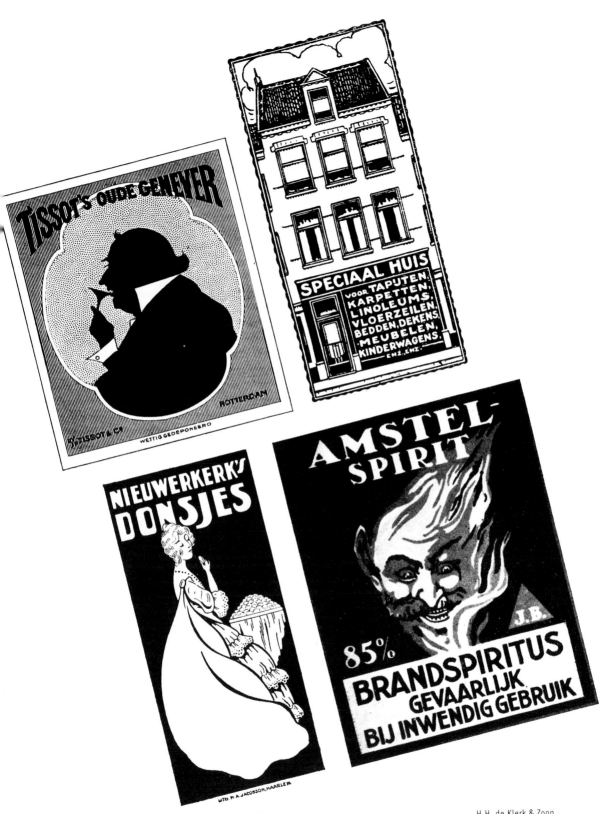

Tissot & Company
Cognac • 1923

P. Nieuwerkerk & Zoon
Cocoa & chocolate • 1924

H.H. de Klerk & Zoon
Carpet & linoleum • 1924

Firma B. Oosterhuis
Methylated spirits • 1923

"Ada"
Dairy products • 1920

V.P.Z.H.
Poultry products • 1927

Cooperative Stoomzuivelfabriek
Milk • 1922

Bergmann & Company
Soap • 1923

J. van Delden
Paints • 1924

Friedrich Klaarenbeck
Pigs & calves • 1927

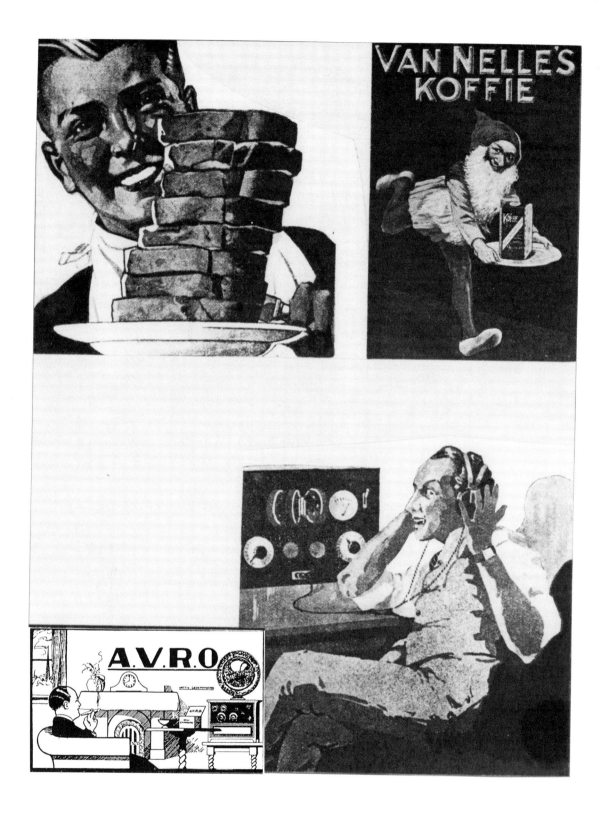

C. Ulrich & Zoon
Bread • 1928

P.D. van Maaren
Tobacco products • 1928

J. van Nelle
Coffee • 1926

Engers & Faber
Writing paper • 1925

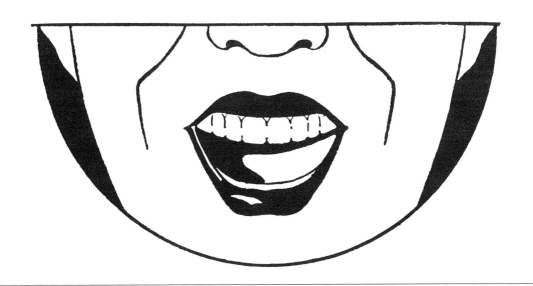

Gerardus Nooy
Confections • 1925

"De Lindeboom"
Biscuits • 1928

H. van Gimborn
Materials for printing • *1925*

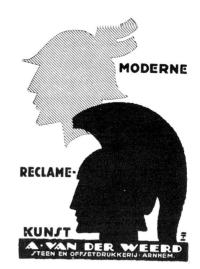

P. van der Sanden
Cigars • 1923

A. van der Weerd
Publicity printer • 1925

A.C. van Oorschot
Cigars • 1927

Louis Dobbelmann
Pipe tobacco • 1926

Theodoor van Buuren
Automobile polish • 1923

Clara Swaab
Furniture polish • 1924

Wijn-Import Maatschappij
Wine imports • 1926

Brinks Theehandel
Coffee • 1924

Dresselhuijs & Nieuwenhuijsen
Cigars • 1925

Gijarth's Sigarenfabrieken
Cigars • 1926

J. Berkers
Cigars • 1928

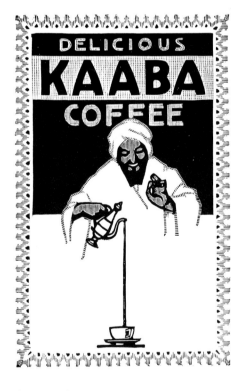

J.M. Huls
Elastic sleeve holders • 1927

P. Broekema
Coffee • 1927

Jacques Antoine Bosmans
Cigars • 1926

Industrie HAG
Coffee • 1924

"De Ooievaar"
Wine & spirits • 1925

Zijlstra Hzn.
Cocoa • 1928

J. van Kregten
Candy • 1929

Bensdorf & Company
Cocoa & chocolate • 1927

Kanis & Gunnink
Coffee & tea • 1926

Kanis & Gunnink
Coffee & tea • 1928

Wed. & Gebrs. Staffhorst
Wine & spirits • 1925

Nederlandsche Chemische Industrie
Glues & adhesives • 1927

Kalker's Modemagazijnen
Manufacturing • 1927

Gebroeders Reijsoo
Manufacturing • 1927

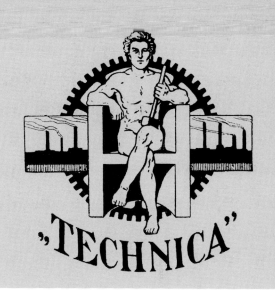

"TECHNICA"

Taconis & Wijnveldt's Stoomtabakskerverij
Tobacco products • 1929

Herman J. de Wolff
Automobiles & motorcycles • 1923

Consumptiefabriek "Brandes"
Food products • 1923

Haagsche Fotobeurs Focusa
Cameras • 1923

Stichting Beheer Vijandelijke
Feed production • 1922

Ernst August Kestein
Bicycles & motorcycles • 1925

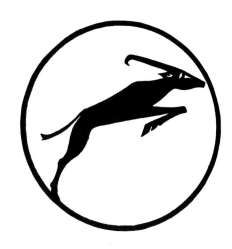

Johan de Heer
Loudspeakers • 1927

Wed. G. Oud & Company
Wine • 1925

Jacob Maartens
Dyes • 1928

Twentsche Oversea Trading Co.
Trading company • 1924

True Tone Company
Phonographs • 1929

Leijtens & Jansen
Transportation vehicles • 1929

Herman Crebas
Tobacco products • 1927

Auto Vrachtbrief
Transport documents • 1933

Staat der Nederlanden
Sulphuric acid • 1926

Nederlandsche Radio Omroep
Radio programming • 1927

R.S. Stokris & Zonen
Radio equipment • 1928

Droste's Chocoladefabrieken
Chocolate label • 1928

Maximiliaan Prins
Eyeglasses • 1924

Bierbrouwerij-Maatschappij
Pilsener beer label • 1924

J.A. Haas & Zonen
Vinegar label • 1927

Handelsonderneming van J. Zijlstra Hzn.
Food labels • 1928

Gebrs. van Leer
Carpets • 1925

W. Hoegee
Bicycles • 1925

Jos. Wolters Jr.
Cigars & cigarettes • 1925

De Erven de Wed. J. van Nelle
Tobacco products label • 1927

J.G. Vos
Construction materials • 1929

Maatschappij tot Exploitatie van een Dagblad
voor Deventer en Omstreken
Raincoats & umbrellas • 1930

S.K. van de Berg
Cigars & cigarettes • 1930

Wed. H. Bontamps
Writing pads • 1928

J.C. van Lieshout & Zoon
Liquids & powders for carpets • 1928

C.J. Kip
Automobile polish • 1927

P. Broekma
Coffee • 1928

Vereenigde Zeepfabrieken
Soap label • 1928

Willem Duijn
Rubber heels & soles • 1930

Karl van Wely
Pipe tobacco • 1928

Karl van Wely
Cigars • 1933

B.J. van 't Oever
Cigars • 1922

P.H. Verseveldt
Cat food • 1926

Vereenigde Zeepfabrieken
Soap & detergent • 1927

Nederlandsche Phoenix
Printed matter • 1927

Lambertus Temmink
Tennis rackets & balls • 1929

Simons & Company
Notepads • 1927

Pharmaceutische Fabriek A. Mijnhardt
Pharmaceuticals • 1929

Nederlandsche Seintoestellen Fabriek
Radios • 1929

Rijk Cornelis Giard
Polishes • 1928

C.J. van Houten & Zoon
Cocoa & chocolate • 1929

Jan van Veen
Mattresses & bedding • 1931

van den Heuvel & Company
Wine • 1928

Alex Israels Corset-Industrie
Corsets • 1930

J. Wolters
Animal food • 1928

Stoomzuivelfabriek "Aurore"
Milk • 1929

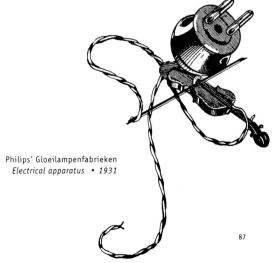

Directeuren Electriciteitsbedrijven
Electrical equipment • *1931*

Nanne Veenstra
Periodical • *1928*

Philips' Gloeilampenfabrieken
Electrical apparatus • *1931*

C.H. Verbeek
Machinery • 1933

van Ankersmit's Katoenfabrieken
Wool & linens • 1929

S.S. Osinga
Tobacco products • 1930

Gebr. van den Bergh's Koninklijke Industrie
Woven kapok • 1932

TTIG GEDEPONEERD

August Bigot & Company
Paper & cartons • 1930

Goemans Warborgt
Food label • 1934

Pieter Adrianus Houberg
Pharmaceuticals • 1930

Petrus Lambertus Taheij
Spices • 1932

H. Hollenkamp & Company
Children's clothing • 1932

Homer van Belle
Wine & apertifs • 1931

S. Bendien & Zonen
Bedding • 1930

Laat van Hooren
Publicity design • 1931

Lens Aandewwiel en Dijk
Fuel • 1930

Nederlandsche Rubberfabrieken
Rubber heels • 1931

C. Simons
Bread • 1932

Uri Cohen
Writing paper • 1932

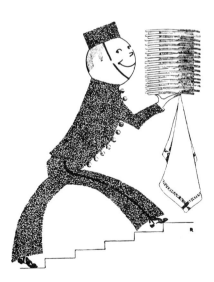

E.L.I.T.E. Elektrische Lampen Industrie
Light bulbs • 1932

Linnenverhuur-Inrichting "Amsterdam"
Linens • 1933

Magazijnen Grand Bazar Francais Galeries Modernes
Chocolates • 1933

Meelfabriek "Kralingen"
Grains • 1932

Cornelis van Steenderen
Handkerchiefs • 1935

Wilhelmus Henricus Kloes
Clotheslines • 1934

W. Peters van Oijen
Fodder • 1933

Maatschappij voor Wasverwerking
Soda • 1938

Cornelis Petrus Theodorus Ebling
Bread & biscuits • 1934

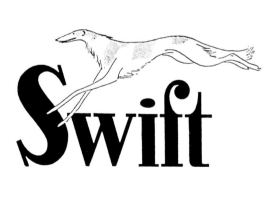

KOKKIE LANGOOR

Wotana Schoenfabriek
Clothing • 1938

Haas' Azijnfabrieken
Food products • 1937

Rubberfabriek "Vredestein"
Shoes • 1934

Dullaert & Company
Buckshot • 1935

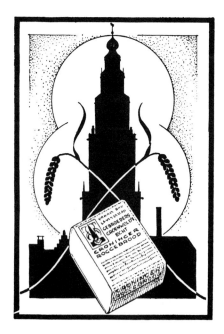

Handels Maatschappij
Yarn • 1934

Gebroeders Groenwald
Bread • 1933

Jan v. d. Hart
Linens & cloth goods • 1934

Repke Faber
Coffee & tea • 1933

"Matheko"
Coffee & tea • 1932

J.C. Dorlas
Coffee & tea • 1932

Vereeniging voor de Theecultuur in Nederlandsche-Indie
Advertising mark to promote tea • 1936

Fertil - Kali
Grain production • 1934

Grete Rosenthal & Company
Scissors • 1936

Schoenfabriek Wellen & Company
Footwear • 1936

Drogerijen Maatschappij
Combs • 1936

Vennootschap Inco Combinatie
Food products • 1936

A. Driessen
Cocoa & chocolate • 1936

S. van Westerborg
Writing papers • 1937

American Lubricating Oils
Industrial oils • 1934

Handel-en Industrie Muj. voor Textiel "Alintex"
Woolen gloves • 1933

L. van Leer & Company
Toys • 1934

De Rotterdamsche Melkinrichting
Milk • 1934

Curt Frankenberg
Tubes • 1934

TARVO MEELFABRIEKEN
HAARLEM

Albert Heijn
Coffee & tea • 1936

"Alpina" Banketfabriek
Pastries • 1935

M.J. Vos
Grain & meal • 1935

Partner

M.J. Vos
Grain & meal • 1934

Stereo Beschuit-en Koekfabrie
Bread & biscuits • 1935

Gebroeders Levie
Overcoats • 1936

Gebroeders Levie
Raincoats • 1936

Tonnema & Company
Chocolates & bonbons • 1932

Colgate-Palmolive N.V.
Toiletries • 1934

Le Roi Soleil
Toiletries • 1935

Emil Heymann
Paints • 1934

Parfumerieen Fabriel
Toiletries • 1941

Herman van Hess
Washing powders • 1936

F.J. Tempel
Coffee • 1939

„Kabouter'

P.C. Schiffelen
Peanut wafers • 1935

Hendrik Elfers
Cheeses • 1936

Schoewen-Industrie
Shoes • 1937

Vorwerk & Company
Polishers • 1936

Ebling & van Spronsen
Bread • 1940

J. de Ruiter
Coffee package • 1937

Vennootschap de Bataafsche Petroleum Maatschappij
Petroleum products • 1936

"Leidsche Wolspinnerij"
Wool • 1937

Bruyns & Company
Pastries • 1938

Arthur Dumoleyn
Beer • 1935

S. van Hessen & Company
Sausages • 1935

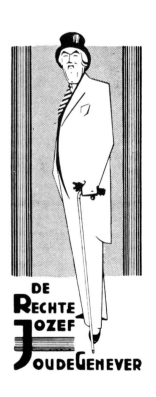

Wijnbedriff Wiro
Wine • 1936

Albino Maatschappij
Food products • 1936

Drogerijen Maatschappij
Hair preparations • 1936

Franciscus Antonius Mols
Spirits • 1937

L.W. van Nieuwenhuyzen
Fruits • 1934

Rubberfabriek "Ceylon"
Articles of rubber • 1937

Maatschappij "De Betuwe"
Food products • 1935

A. Hillen's Tabaksfabriek
Cigars • 1935

G.J. van Gelder
Peas • 1935

TOON KOFFER

Import Maatschappij
Washing machines • 1938

N.V. Distilleerderij
Soft drinks • 1939

H.W.M. Domensino
Milk • 1938

H.H. Kolthof
Clothing • 1940

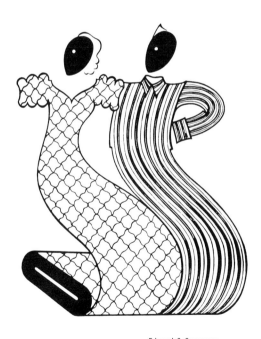

Gasfabrikanten in Nederland
Gas industry • 1938

Woldring & Idema
Wines • 1942

Eduard & Company
Industrial chemicals • 1938

Vlissingen & Company
Fabrics • 1937

Waschproductenfabriek Loda
Polishes • 1939

Louis Dobbelmann
Tobacco products • 1937

Hendrik Jansen
Antifreeze • 1939

Gerson Levie
Baking goods • 1935

Fr. van Gelder
Foot care preparations • 1936

W. van Amerongen
Food products • 1936

Hermann Schreuder & Company
Paint • 1938

J.L.A. Heygele
Wristwatches • 1938

Deutz Oliehandel
Insecticide • 1937

Dethmer Schuitema
Colonial products • 1939

PERFECTA

N.V. BIERBROUWERIJ
›DE VRIENDENKRING‹

Nederlandsche Rubberfabrieken
Rubber tires • 1937

Handelsonderneming van de Reepe
Glue & adhesives • 1938

J. Veldkamp
Cheeses • 1935

Stoombierbrouwerij De Vriendenkring
Beer • 1936

Centrale Suiker Maatschappij
Food product labels • 1937

St. Martinus
Milk • 1939

Johann Mullaart
Stencils & duplicating machines • 1937

Dalenoord & Company
Brie • 1938

Chemische Industrie "Azinol"
Detergent • 1941

WETTIG
GEDEPONEERD

M. Jansen-de Wit's Kousenfabrieken
Stockings • 1939

P. Mars & Company
Household products • 1930

Nederlandsche Linoleumfabriek
Linoleum • 1938

"De Volharding"
Milk • 1940

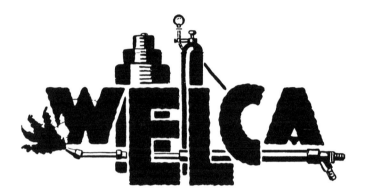

H. Vettewinkel & Zonen
Lacquer • 1941

"Nimco"
Shoes • 1935

"Het Handelswapen"
Business machines • 1939

Freidrich Weller
Welding equipment • 1941

Bouwmaterialenhandel Treetex
Fiberboards • 1936

J.C. Keg & Company
Cheese • 1940

Th. J.L. van den Berg
Fire resistant coverings • 1939

A.J.H. Rooymans
Cigars • 1937

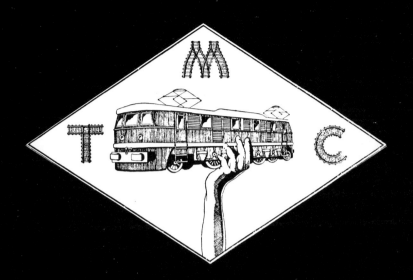

Cornelius Harman Gerlings
Toy trains • 1942

Diopha
Vitamins • 1941

OLVEH van 1879

LEVENSVERZEKERING

Het Ouderling
Polishes • 1941

Biscuitfabriek "Victoria"
Biscuits & pastries • 1941

Collopharma
Powdered drinks • 1941

Saccharinefabriek "Hollandia"
Artificial sweeteners • 1939

Paul C. Kaiser
Bread & biscuits • 1939

Lonneker Cooperative Melkinrichting en Zuivelfabriek
Milk • 1941

S. Kuperus
Mattresses • 1942

Chemische Industrie "Corona"
Essences for food • 1944

A. de Geus van den Heuvel
Household products • 1942

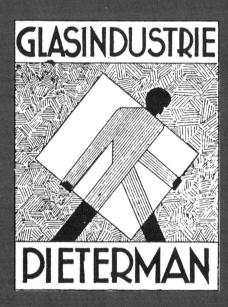

Glasindustrie Pieterman
Plate glass • 1941

J.W.J. van der Zanden
Paper & cartons • 1942

Heldersche Melkcentrale
Milk • 1943

B. Baur & Zoon
Milk • 1942

Cooperative Fabriek van
Melkproducten voor de Neder-Betuwe
Milk • 1947

Leidsche Melkinrichting
Milk • 1942

A. Kool
Milk • 1940

Radio Apparat Company
Radio apparatus • 1942

J. van der Hoeden
Chocolate • 1943

"Alroha"
Baked goods • 1941

Hendrik Bakker
Grain production • 1945

Otten & Company
Clothing • 1943

Otten & Company
Clothing • 1943

Vennootschap Emdi
Agricultural transport • 1943

"De Mutator"
Printed material • 1944

Gebroeders Laan
Grain production • 1943

Transformatoren- en Apparatenfabriek "De Drie"
Electric transformers • 1943

Zilverfabriek A. Mesker & Zoon
Silver fabrication • 1944

H. E. Sipkes
Food products • 1943

H.A. Mensing
Lemonade • 1945

A. Barreveld
Grain production • 1946

Frank Rijsdijk
Metals • 1942

"Columbus"
Baked goods • 1942

"Impac"
Glass products • 1945

Cornelis Harman Gerlings
Bicycles • 1944

Vroom & Dreesmann
Paper & cartons • 1941

J.P. Wyers
Bedding • 1938

Keip-Optiek
Eyeglasses • 1941

Kristalunie Maatstricht
Products in crystal • 1938

H.W. Hofland
Postage stamps • 1944

F. Verschoor
Stationery supplies • 1946

Vitam Vruchtenproducten
Apple juice • 1946

Faddegon & Company
Playing cards • 1943

C.E. Valanidas
Coffee & tea extract • 1940

J. Westerman & Company
Coffee, tea & cocoa • 1942

Erve J. van den Bergh
Coffee & tea • 1943

Nederlandsche Stoombleekerij
Cotton • 1941

Uitgeverij Contact
Book publishers • 1947

J.M. van Haeften
Hearing aids • 1941

M.F. Ternbach
Cigarette papers • 1945

Rubberhandel P.S. Bakker
Rubber products • 1944

"Waldorp"
Instruments • 1944

Heineken's Bierbrouwerij
Alcoholic beverage • 1947

P.L. Kerkvliet
Clothing • 1940

Kalmar & Kremer
Machinery • 1947

B. van Ballegooijen
Milk • 1946

G. Peeters
Poultry • 1949

H. Evenblij
Industrial containers • 1946

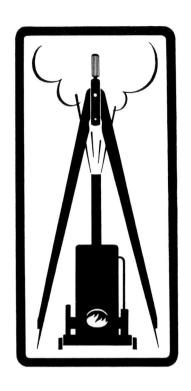

"Fototypie"
Technical instruments • 1945

J. Kleinbussink & Zoon
Machinery • 1943

Koolborstelfabriek Holland
Electrical apparatus • 1944

P. Planken
Firefighting equipment • 1944

De Bond van Bloembollenhandelaren
Tulip bulbs • 1946

W. Bos
Meat products • 1947

Chemische Fabriek "Ophir"
Perfume & cosmetics • 1945

Parfumerie Groothandel
Perfume & cosmetics • 1947

"Actief"
Labels • 1947

J. Schoenmakers
Wood for construction • 1947

J.J. Staekenborg
Cosmetics • 1947

N.V. Intermetaal
Steel production • 1949

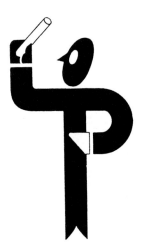

B. SMIT

Nieuwstadt Technisch Bureau
Radio equipment • 1947

Pharmachemie
Pharmaceuticals • 1945

B. Smit
Food products • 1945

Voedingsproducten Vlevo
Bouillon • 1947

Publiciteits 't Raedthuys
Publicity design • 1946

Maatschappij "Senzora"
Paint & paintbrushes • 1949

Bedrijven Mammora N.V.
Machinery • 1946

Mazereeuw"s Zaad- en
Pootaardappelenhandel
Agricultural products • 1949

Niemeijers
TABAK

H. Bootz' Distilleerderij
Wine & beer • 1948

Th. W. Frumau
Leathergoods • 1949

Theodorus Niemeijer
Tobacco products • 1949

"Ria"
Raincoats • 1946

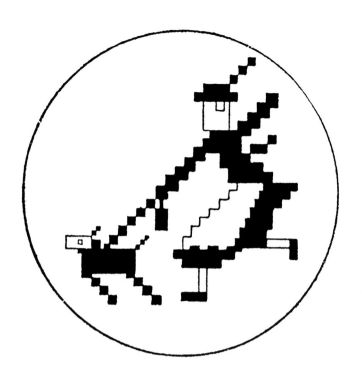

Klaas Fuite
Floor coverings • 1950

Claus' Garen- en Weefindustrie
Textiles • 1949

Tricotagefabriek Evana
Tricots • 1950

Bergings- en Transportbedriff
Steamer transport • 1949

Maatschappij "Nutricia"
Milk • 1949

Chemische Fabriek C. Dolfin
Bleach • 1945

Zuid-Nederlandsche Zuivelbond
Butter • 1949

Gebroeders Bouhuys
Petroleum imports • *1948*

Buhrmann's Papiergroothandel
Paper & cartons • 1949

Germoco N.V.
Lubricating oil • 1950

I.L. Spreekmeester
Pencils • 1949

The **Exlibris,** or bookplate, has been a common identifying mark for **book** owners throughout history. Use of these expressive graphic designs dates from the 1700s in the Netherlands, reflecting the personalities of the artists and individuals for whom they were created. In the 1920s and 1930s, the exlibris became highly stylized, generally utilizing woodcuts or engravings to symbolize the book owner's profession or social/political interests. Although technically not considered trademark designs, these graphic images evolved into personal logos which communicate in much the same manner as a symbol does for a business. It is probable that some exlibris artists were also trademark designers, as similarities are apparent in the quality of the preceding logos and that of the exlibris designs of the same period. The selections reproduced are just a few examples from <u>Tweehonderd Nederlandse Grafische Kunstnaars</u>, a 1954 book by Johan Schwencke.

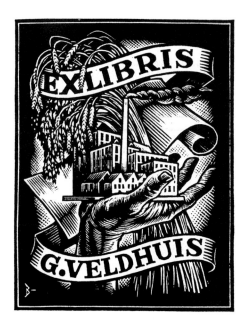

Han Krug

Hil Bottema

Nico Bulder

Anton Pieck

H.D. Voss

Herman Heuff

Anton Pieck

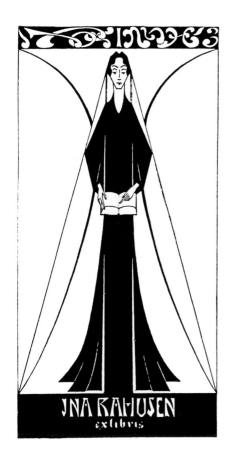

J.F.E. ten Klooster

J.A. Deodatus

Joan Collette

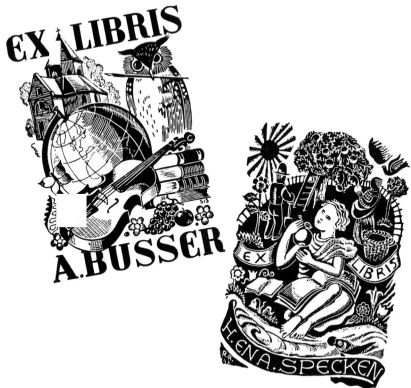

J. van Hell

W.A. van de Walle

Pater Renald Rats

Jan de Cler

Johan Melse

M.C. Escher

Henri Friedlaender

Jac. B. Knol   Johan Melse

Jan Heyse   Georg Rueter

CHARISIUS

G.M. Altena

Johan Dijkstra

Pam Rueter